HOW TO KNOW THE WILL OF GOD

Metropolitan Youssef

How to Know the Will of God
By Metropolitan Youssef

Copyright © 2025 Coptic Orthodox Diocese of the Southern U.S.A.

All rights reserved.

Designed & Published by:
St. Mary & St. Moses Abbey Press
101 S Vista Dr, Sandia, TX 78383
stmabbeypress.com

All Scripture quotations in the footnotes of this book, unless otherwise indicated, are taken from the New King James Version® Copyright © 1982 by Thomas Nelson, Inc. Used by permission. All rights reserved.

The following Septuagint text is used when indicated: *The Septuagint Version of the Old Testament*. (London, UK: Samuel Bagster and Sons, 1879).

Contents

Chapter One
Why is it Important to Discover the Will of God?   5

Chapter Two
Types of the Will of God   9

Chapter Three
Principles on the Will of God   20

Chapter Four
Means to Discover the Will of God   25

Chapter Five
How to Know the Will of God   29

Chapter Six
Concluding Remarks   42

Guiding Questions for Reflection   46

Questions and Answers   48

1

Why is it Important to Discover the Will of God?

God has a perfect plan for each person

Why is it important to know the will of God—to discover His will? You should know that God has a plan: in Jeremiah it says, "For I know the thoughts that I think toward you, says the Lord, thoughts of peace and not of evil, to give you a future and a hope."[1] God is speaking to us, "I know the thoughts that I, God, think about you," so God has a wonderful plan for each one of us. When He created us, even before our creation, He had a plan for each one of us, and this plan is a plan of peace, not of evil, to give us a future and a hope. Like a father—all of our

---

1   Jeremiah 29:11.

parents wish the best for us—, God our heavenly Father wants the best for us, and He has a plan. God wants His will to be perfectly accomplished in our life. Why? Is it to have control? Is it because God is a controlling God? No. He wants His plan to be perfectly accomplished in our life, because this is what will give us joy and happiness and peace in our life. And when we fall out of His plan, that is when we begin to suffer. In the epistle of St. Paul to the Colossians, he says, "Always laboring fervently for you in prayers, that you may stand perfect and complete in all the will of God."[2] So Epaphras was praying for the people of Colossi fervently that they may stand perfect and complete in all the will of God. Why? Because this will give us peace and joy and happiness in our life.

The Lord Jesus Christ obeyed the will of the Father

As an example we have our Lord Jesus Christ. He came to do the will of God the Father. As we read in the gospel of St. John, the Lord said, "My food is to do the will of Him who sent Me."[3] What is the meaning of "My food is to do the will of Him"? It means that when we do the will of God, we will be nourished and nurtured, which is what the Lord Jesus Christ said about His relationship with the Father.

---

2 Colossians 4:12.

3 John 4:34.

My food is to do the will of Him—the Father—who sent Me. The Lord also said, "I do not seek My own will but the will of the Father who sent Me."[4] And in His prayer in the garden of Gethsemane, He said, "Father, if it is Your will, take this cup away from Me; nevertheless not My will, but Yours, be done."[5] Here the Lord Jesus Christ gave us an example of how He came to do the will of the Father.

St. Mary obeyed the will of God

Likewise the Church uses St. Mary as an example for us. So why did God choose St. Mary to be His mother? Because she did the will of God. The gospel says that His brothers and His mother came and were standing outside. They sent to Him, calling Him. And a multitude was standing around Him. Someone said to Him, "Look, Your mother and Your brothers are outside seeking You."[6] But He answered them, saying, "'Who is My mother, or My brothers?' And He looked around in a circle at those who sat about Him, and said, 'Here are My mother and My brothers! For whoever does the will of God is My brother and My sister and mother.'"[7] The Lord is telling us who His mother is. Why did God choose St. Mary out of all the women of the world, to be

---

4 John 5:30.
5 Luke 22:42.
6 Mark 3:32.
7 Mark 3:33–35.

His mother? Because she did the will of God. So, if we do the will of God, we will be in the family of God, as He said: for whoever does the will of God is My brother and My sister and mother. I can have the same relationship, as St. Mary was to God; I can have the same relationship if I keep and do the will of God. All that you need is that you do the will of God in your life, like St. Mary. When archangel Gabriel announced to her the Good News, she said to him, "Behold the maidservant of the Lord! Let it be to me according to your word."[8] St. Mary submitted her will completely—denied her will completely—to [do] the will of God.

---

[8] Luke 1:38.

2

Types of the Will of God

The general will of God

There are some points I would like to highlight. First, there is what we call the general will of God, meaning the will of God for all of us. As we read in the Scripture, "In everything give thanks; for this is the will of God in Christ Jesus for you."[9] God wants us to be thankful, to be grateful; this is the will of God. Also, in the same epistle, St. Paul said, "For this is the will of God, your sanctification: that you should abstain from sexual immorality."[10] This is the will of God: to be holy, specifically you abstain from sexual immorality.

Also, another example for the general will of God can be found in the first epistle of St. Peter:

---

9   1 Thessalonians 5:18.
10 1 Thessalonians 4:3.

"For this is the will of God, that by doing good you may put to silence the ignorance of foolish men."[11] God want you to do good; that is the will of God.

The will of God is that we hold fast to the sound doctrine. It is the will of God that we abide in the true doctrine, in the sound teaching of the Church, because when we drift away from the sound teaching, this technically will affect our sanctification. In his epistle to the Romans, St. Paul said, "I urge you, brethren, note those who cause divisions and offenses, contrary to the doctrine which you learned, and avoid them."[12] Unfortunately, right now many people are not careful about the sound doctrine. We see many people—and sometimes unfortunately even Sunday school servants—who do not mind to go from one denomination to another, to attend the Liturgy here, but they attend bible study with non-orthodox people, and so on. But St. Paul made it clear that you need to avoid those who are teaching contrary to the doctrine which you learned; this is the will of God. We never heard, for example, St. John the beloved, who is known for his meekness and his humbleness, speak very assertively as when he spoke about false teachers. We read in his epistles, that he said that if anyone comes to you not with this doctrine, do not greet him, do not receive him in your house, because if you greet him or receive him in your house, you are participating in his evil

---

11   1 Peter 2:15.

12   Romans 16:17.

words.[13] So the apostle who spoke about love said that when it comes to the doctrine, to the teaching, "No, you cannot compromise this. You need to take a stand, you need to say 'No,' you do not interact with them or attend activities with them." Here St. Paul is very clear: those who are teaching contrary to the doctrine which you learned, you need to avoid them; this is the will of God.

In the epistle of St. Peter we learn about another general will of God, another common will of God to all of us: obedience to the commandments of God even the commandments that are against our own will. True obedience is when you obey something that is against your own will, because if you obey only when it goes with your own will, this is not obedience; you are doing your own will. This catholic epistle gives us the example of Sarah the wife of Abraham. The point of submission is extremely difficult for all of us because of our pride, because of our ego. We find it difficult to submit to our fathers. We find it difficult to submit to our parents. Wives usually find it difficult to submit to their husbands. The will of God is that wives submit to their husbands, and perhaps this is against our own will, but in the catholic epistle, St. Peter says, "Wives, likewise, be submissive to your own husbands, that even if some do not obey the word, they, without a word, may be won by the conduct

---

13   See 2 John 1:10.

of their wives."[14] St. Peter is saying that you need to submit to your husband, even if he does not obey the word of God; and when you submit, you will win him over. And he continues by saying, "When they observe your chase conduct and accompanied by fear."[15] After this he says, "For in this manner, in former times, the holy women who trusted in God also adorned themselves, being submissive to their own husbands, as Sarah obeyed Abraham, calling him lord, whose daughters you are if you do good and are not afraid with any terror."[16] We read this part during the crowning ceremony; and unfortunately in many weddings that I have attended, when this part is read, people laugh and take it lightly as if we were saying a joke, not knowing that these are the words of the Holy Spirit; we are reading from the Scriptures, so these words should be taken seriously. We are not joking here: this is the will of God. When we apply the will of God, we do so because we trust in God, and we trust that if others, to whom we submit, start to take advantage of this, God will defend us as He defended Sarah and said to Abraham that whatever Sarah tells you, do for her. This is why, St. Peter highlighted the trust of the holy women of God, the women who trusted God.

Also, the will of God for husbands is to love their wives, as Christ loved the church and laid His life

---

14   1 Peter 3:1.

15   1 Peter 3:2.

16   1 Peter 3:5–6.

for her. This is the will of God for husbands. That is why he said, "Husbands, likewise, dwell with them with understanding, giving honor to the wife."[17] The fact that the Lord said to the wives "submit your husbands," this does not give the husband the right to dishonor his wife, but rather to honor her and to appreciate her, to dwell with her with understanding, knowing the delicate nature of women, because God made them equal to the husbands in heaven, as St. Peter said, "As being heirs together of the grace of life."[18] Therefore, when God said "submit," He is not putting them in a lower status. It is just for the regulation, for the order. Somebody has to be a leader, but do not misinterpret the virtue of submission, as though women were less than men or lower than men. Husbands need to honor them because they are equal partakers and inheritors of the grace of life; and then he said, "That your prayers may not be hindered."[19] If you do not love your wife, if you do not honor her, if you do not consider her equal to you in the grace of life, then your prayers will be hindered. God will not listen to your prayers. This is the will of God. The will of God is to obey the commandment of God, even if it is against our own will, even if it is difficult for me as a wife to submit to my own husband, even if it is difficult for me as a husband to honor my

---

17 1 Peter 3:7.
18 Ibid.
19 Ibid.

wife and put her ahead of me. But that is the will of God. And if you want to be like St. Mary, then you need to do the will of God. St. Mary was submissive to Joseph, and she obeyed him, and she listened to him. And when Joseph thought that her pregnancy was out of sin, God defended her, because she put her trust in God.

St. Paul told us that the will of God is to abide in the sound doctrine and to avoid those who are teaching what is contrary to it. St. Peter said that the will of God is to obey His commandments, even the commandments that are against our own will or the ones we find difficult to keep. The Book of Acts says that the will of God is to carry the cross and to suffer for His name. When Agabus the prophet took St. Paul's belt, he said, "Thus says the Holy Spirit, 'So shall the Jews at Jerusalem bind the man who owns this belt, and deliver him into the hands of the Gentiles.'"[20] Agabus was saying that St. Paul would be delivered to the hands of the Gentiles, and would be tortured, and would suffer there. So this is the will of God; this is what the Holy Spirit said. But his friends, because they loved him, were trying to convince St. Paul not to go to Jerusalem. St. Paul, however, answered and said to them, "What do you mean by weeping and breaking my heart? For I am ready not only to be bound, but also to

---

20   Acts 21:11.

die at Jerusalem for the name of the Lord Jesus."[21] Therefore, when they saw his determination to suffer for the name of Christ, all of them said, "The will of the Lord be done."[22] This is the will of God: to suffer for His name. "For to you it has been granted on behalf of Christ, not only to believe in Him, but also to suffer for His sake."[23]

It is the will of God to obey His commandments, even the commandments that we feel to be difficult. It is the will of God for us to abide in the sound doctrine and the sound teaching. This is the will of God in our life, what we call the common will of God for everyone. Any believer should abide by these: to suffer for His name, to obey His commandments, to avoid those who are teaching wrong doctrine and wrong teaching, to pursue sanctification, to do good, to give thanks in everything.

The specific or personal will of God

The aforementioned is what we call the general will of God for all of us, but there is a specific will of God. For example, which career do I pursue, which college do I enroll in, which person do I marry, which job do I apply for, which house or city do I live in? Of course you cannot find a verse in the Bible that would tell you, "Do this." Sometimes

---

21 Acts 21:13.

22 Acts 21:14.

23 Philippians 1:29.

we wish or we hope that we know the will of God through a dream, or that we see a vision, or that we see archangel Gabriel coming to us and telling us, "Do this; this is the will of God in your life." But unfortunately this rarely happens, so we need to be persistent in seeking the will of God. When we are persistence and seeking His will and seeking His guidance, He told us, "Ask, and you will receive."[24] Also, the Lord said to us, "Seek first the kingdom of God and His righteousness, and all these things shall be added to you."[25] This means that if you seek the kingdom of God and His righteousness, if you live righteously, God will reveal to you in a way or another His will in everything else. Seek first the kingdom of God and His righteousness and all these things will be added to you. And here is the rule, one rule that is very important: if you are faithful and honest in keeping the general will of God— to do good, sanctification, abstain from sexual immorality, giving thanks in everything—if you are faithful in this area, then God will reveal to you His will in other areas. But if you are not faithful but are careless about fulfilling the will of God in this general area, why would God reveal to you His will in other areas. So, the more you are faithful, the more the will of God will be revealed to you regarding the specific questions.

God knows that the process of seeking Him is

---

24 John 16:24.
25 Matthew 6:33.

very important, which is the answer that He might give to any question. So, when you take steps of faith, and when you learn to recognize His will, and when you grow spiritually, and when you strengthen your relationship with Him, then it will be easy for you to recognize His will. St. Paul in his epistle to the Colossians prayed a beautiful prayer that people may know the will of God:

> For this reason we also, since the day we heard it, do not cease to pray for you, and to ask that you may be filled with the knowledge of His will in all wisdom and spiritual understanding; that you may walk worthy of the Lord, fully pleasing Him, being fruitful in every good work and increasing in the knowledge of God.[26]

I differentiated between the general will of God and the specific will of God, but there is also another classification. The other classification is the sovereign will of God and the prescriptive will of God.

The sovereign will of God

Briefly, sovereign means that this is the will of God that will happen no matter what. When God states that something will happen, it will. No one can

---

26 Colossians 1:9–10.

stop His sovereign will. Here is an example: in His economy, that God would send His Son, our Lord Jesus Christ, to die on the cross for the sins of the world. This was the will of God, and this was going to happen no matter what. This is what we call the sovereign will of God. Knowing about the sovereign will of God gives us comfort in our hearts, because no matter what we do, no matter what others will do, we cannot ruin God's ultimate plan. When king Saul pursued David to kill him, David said to Saul, "If God gave you permission to kill me, let it be so; let Him accept a sacrifice. If God did not give you permission to kill me, you cannot kill me."[27] Therefore, in the time of uncertainty you can remember God's sovereign will, that once you are His child, the child of God, nothing can separate you from His love—that is, His will. If you choose to be His son, nothing will separate you from His love. As we read in the epistle to the Romans, "For I am persuaded that neither death nor life, nor angels nor principalities nor powers, nor things present nor things to come, nor height nor depth, nor any other created thing, shall be able to separate us from the love of God which is in Christ Jesus our Lord."[28]

The prescriptive will of God

What about the prescriptive will of God? Prescriptive

---

27 See 1 Samuel 26:18–20.
28 Romans 8:38–39.

comes from the word prescription. It is what God is asking us to do. God gave us a commandment, but He also gave us choice. He gave a commandment to Adam and Eve, "Do not eat of this tree," but they had a choice—choice whether to obey His commandments or not. So God asks us to pray without ceasing; God asks us to love one another, to forgive one other. This is His will for you, but again at the end it is your choice. Understanding the character of God through His word and through His commandments will enable us to seek His will in other situations. For example, God wants me to pray without ceasing. If you choose a job in a city where there is no church in it, and the closest church is ten hours away from you, if you think about it, no, this is not the will of God. How can I take a job in a place where I cannot worship Him, neither I nor my family. Here is another example: if I choose a person who is not Christian and I want to marry this person, how can we become one in Jesus Christ. How can the Holy Spirit unite both of us? This is definitely not the will of God. That is to say, when I understand His commandments, then this will help me to seek His will in any other situation. At the end, you have a choice to obey or disobey Him. You can choose to take this job or not. You can choose to marry this person or not. Know this, however, that my disobedience to the will of God will not affect God's ultimate plan, but rather it will hurt me. I will be hurt if I do not follow His will.

3

Principles on the Will of God

Willingness to do His will even before we know it

There are important and quick principles. The first principle is that if you really want to discover the will of God, you must be willing to do His will even before you know what it is. If you are not willing to do it, God will not feed your curiosity to merely let you discover His will, only because you are curious to know it and that is it. In the gospel of St. John, the Lord said, "If anyone wills to do His will, he shall know concerning the doctrine, whether it is from God or whether I speak on My own authority."[29] So, the Lord is saying that when we know the will of God, we should be willing to do it. The Jews rejected the Lord Jesus Christ and

---

29 John 7:17.

rejected His doctrine, so the Lord said, "If you want to do His will, then you will not reject Me, you will not reject My will, you will not reject My doctrine like the Jews; you will be willing to do them." So the first principle is that if you want to discover the will of God, you need to be willing to do it, no matter what.

God is not an author of confusion

Another principle is that God is not an author of confusion. That is to say, God will not send you a certain message through the Scriptures, a different message in your heart, a third message through your father of confession, a forth message through your parents, a fifth message through your friends, and so on. God is not an author of confusion. So, if it is the will of God, God will change the heart of everyone, almost to be in consensus, to declare that this is the will of God, except if some people are clearly against His will; and this will be outside our calculation. But anybody who is willing wholeheartedly to know the will of God, all will be in agreement: whether you read in the Scripture, or the voice in your heart, or the counseling you are receiving from your spiritual father, or you hear from your parents; everything will be in harmony together.

Having a fellowship with the Lord

A third principle is simply the following: It is our daily or hourly fellowship with the Lord. As we will discuss later, God will guide us like the GPS. When you are driving, you must keep your eyes on the GPS. If you do not keep your eyes on the GPS, you will be lost. In the same way you need to keep your eyes on God. God will instruct and teach you. Therefore, if God is to guide us, then we must first focus our eyes on Him, to look to Him regularly throughout the day, to have this fellowship with Him from minute to minute.

At all time God is preparing and directing us toward His will

God will both prepare and direct us for whatever He has in His mind, even if He does not reveal it to us. In the Second Book of Samuel, David the prophet said, "God is my strength and power, and He makes my way perfect."[30] He prepares and directs my steps. Also, in Hebrews, St. Paul says:

> Now may the God of peace who brought up our Lord Jesus from the dead, that great Shepherd of the sheep, through the blood of the everlasting covenant, make you complete in every good work to do His will, working

---

30   2 Samuel 22:33.

in you what is well pleasing in His sight, through Jesus Christ, to whom be glory forever and ever. Amen.[31]

Therefore, it is God who will make you complete in every good work in order to do His will, working in you to do what is well pleasing in His sight.

The peace of God is a strong indicator that you are walking in His will

When God is leading me, one of the sure signs that I am walking according to His will is the peace. His peace will rule in my heart even if I am in prison like St. Paul, even if I am in the lions' den like Daniel, even If I am in the furnace of fire like the three young men; nevertheless, I will have peace. Lack of peace is an important indicator that what we are pursuing may not be the will of God or perhaps it is not God's time yet. So, the peace, in spite of all circumstances, the peace that comes from within, is an indicator that this is the will of God. As St. Paul said, "And let the peace of God rule in your hearts, to which also you were called in one body; and be thankful."[32]

---

31 Hebrews 13:20–21.
32 Colossians 3:15.

God may lead us one step at a time

Also, God may lead us one step at a time. We often do not understand the big picture. The big picture is not revealed yet. When God takes me one step only, at this moment I will be confused concerning what God wants from me, but in spite of this I will have peace. As we read in the Book of Isaiah, "Your ears shall hear a word behind you, saying, 'This is the way, walk in it,' whenever you turn to the right hand or whenever you turn to the left."[33]

So these are several important principles on the will of God: to be willing to do His will no matter what it is; God is not an author of confusion: what you read in His word will be in harmony with what you hear from your father of confession; and you will have peace in your heart; God Himself directs you toward His will and might lead you one step at a time; also you need to be in fellowship with God and to walk with Him all day long, if you want to discover His will.

---

33 Isaiah 30:21.

4

Means to Discover the Will of God

God-given Wisdom

Some of us would perhaps say, "We know the will of God, but we cannot apply it," or others would say, "Wisdom is required to discover the will of God." Yes, but God who has a plan for you, for future and hope, a plan for peace and not evil, God also is willing to give you the wisdom that you need, not only to discover His will but also to execute it in your life. St. James says, "If any of you lacks wisdom, let him ask of God, who gives to all liberally and without reproach, and it will be given to him."[34] Do you need wisdom to know the will of God? Ask for it, and you will receive it. Also, God

---
34   James 1:5.

Himself, speaking to us in psalm 32, says, "I will instruct you and teach you in the way you should go."[35] When God said I will instruct you, it means He is not giving us a direction, but—I apologize for the comparison—He is like a GPS. What do I mean? Before the GPS, if I wanted to come and visit you, you would give me direction: take this highway, and then exit through that exit, and then turn right at such a traffic light, and turn left at that stop sign, and so on. And as I follow the directions, if I missed the exit, I might be lost for an hour. But God, when He told us "I will instruct you and teach you in the way that you should go," He is holding my hand, walking with me step by step; and if I miss the direction, He will re-guide me. Like rerouting, He will redirect me to the right way. In the psalms it says, "Good and upright is the Lord; therefore He will instruct sinners in the way."[36] God will guide those who miss the way; therefore, even when we miss the way, God will guide us.

The Holy Scriptures

God will lead you to discover His will through many channels. One channel is the Scripture, the word of God. In the Book of Isaiah, it says, "To the law and to the testimony! If they do not speak according to this

---

35 Psalms 32:8.
36 Psalms 24:8 LXX.

word, it is because there is no light in them."[37] So if you do not say "to the law and to the testimony," if you do not make the word of God your reference in every decision you make, then there is no light in you.

Opening and Closing Doors

Also, another channel through which God guides us is opening and closing doors for us. He will close certain doors and will open other doors. As we read in the Book of Proverbs, "In all your ways acknowledge Him, and He shall direct your paths."[38] How will He direct it? He will open certain doors and will close others. I will give you an example of how God did this with St. Paul. Also, God prepared and directed St. Paul. I mean, in the upbringing of St. Paul even before his conversion, God was preparing and directing him to this great mission, by making him a disciple of Gamaliel, by making him join the sect of the Pharisees. All these were steps to the great mission. We may not understand all the steps; nevertheless, we should trust that God does not do anything haphazardly.

The Counsel of Others

As we have said, the Scripture is one channel to know His will; another is through opening and closing doors;

---

37 Isaiah 8:20.
38 Proverbs 3:6.

and yet another is through seeking counseling, seeking guidance from mature godly Christians, from our spiritual father, from those who have submitted their will to the will of God. As we read in the Book of Proverbs, "In the multitude of counselors there is safety."[39] Therefore, one channel is the Scripture. Another channel is my spiritual father. A third channel is the godly friends in my life. A fourth channel is the Church Fathers. So all these, and the voice of the Holy Spirit within me, are different channels that will help me to know the will of God.

Affirmative Signs

Although we do not rely on signs, especially a supernatural sign, often God sends us signs that will help us know whether this is the way or not. Like in the Book of Judges Gideon asked for a sign, but this sign was a supernatural sign. He asked God to have the dew be only on the fleece and not on the ground, and then he asked for the opposite. Believe me that many people share with me stories of how God confirmed their decision through one sign or another. And let me assure you that there is nothing happening by coincidence in our life. If you walk out of church or work, and you meet somebody, meeting this person is not by coincidence. Nothing happens by coincidence in our life; therefore, look for or seek information from signs sent by God. And God will send you many signs to confirm His will.

---

[39] Proverbs 11:14.

5

How to Know the Will of God

We will discuss nine practical steps to help us discover the will of God.

1. Walk with God

Walk with God. God will not reveal His will to somebody who is away from Him. You need to develop a relationship with Him. Christianity is about having a relationship, unity, oneness with God. It is not a set of rules and laws you fulfill. It is a relationship with God, and this is the mystery of the incarnation. Why did God become man? Because our transformation will come not through set of laws which we need to follow, but our transformation will come from this union with God. You must therefore cultivate your relationship with God, you must seek to know Him from day to day; spend time in His word, spend time in prayer; take every opportunity to be involved in the church, take every opportunity to be active; the sacraments of the church, fasts of the church—all these disciplines are very important to know the will of God. As we read in the Book of Proverbs, "Trust in the LORD with all your heart, and lean not on your own understanding; in all your ways acknowledge Him, and He shall direct your paths."[40] So, when you trust in God and you do not lean on your own understanding, then in all ways He will direct you and guide you, in every step in your life.

2. Surrender your will to God's will

Surrender your will to God's will as I said before. Frequently when I say I want to discover the will of God, I mean that I want God to do my will for me. Someone might say, "Please pray for me that God may help in this or that"; "pray for me that I may join this school"; "pray for me that I may marry this girl or that boy." I made a decision, and I want God just to execute it for me. In his epistle to the Romans, St. Paul says:

> I beseech you therefore, brethren, by the mercies of God, that you present your bodies a living sacrifice, holy, acceptable to God, which is your reasonable service. And do not be conformed to this world, but be

---

40 Proverbs 3:5–6.

transformed by the renewing of your mind, that you may prove what is that good and acceptable and perfect will of God.[41]

"Presenting your body a living sacrifice," it is self-denial, meaning that you sacrifice yourself on the altar of love, the love of God. I need to offer myself as a sacrifice; I need to renew my mind to have the mind of Christ. Then I will be able to know the will of God, which is perfect, holy, good, acceptable. If God died for us, should we not be willing to live for Him and surrender ourselves to Him, to His will?

Also, unreserved surrender is needed. To know the will of God, you need to be completely willing to deny your own will. A major obstacle in discovering the will of God is that I want my will to be done. Therefore, we must be completely open to whatever God wants. And the best way to do it is to have no will of your own no matter what. This is what the Lord said, "If anyone desires to come after Me, let him deny himself, and take up his cross daily, and follow Me."[42] "Deny himself" means to deny his own will.

There are often two types of prayer. In the first type, I make the decision, and I want God to do it for me. So in a way I am saying to God, "My will be

---

41 Romans 12:1–2.
42 Luke 9:23.

done. God, I want this to happen to me; do it." And if God did not do it, then I would ask and wonder, "Why does God not answer our prayers?" But, you see, in this prayer I made the decision and I want God to execute it for me. The right way of prayer, the second type, is to ask God, "What do You want me to do? I am here to do Your will." This is the prayer of St. Paul before his conversion when he met the Lord on the road to Damascus. He asked God, "Lord, what do You want me to do?"[43]

3. Obey the will of God which you already know

Also, obey what you already know to be the will of God. Almost 98% of His will is already revealed to us in the Scriptures. If you are not following this 98%, why would God reveal to you the remaining 2%? St. Paul says, "For this is the will of God, your sanctification."[44] God wants you not to lie, not to swear, not to curse, not to judge. God wants you to forgive, to be humble, to serve all; and to be the last of all. God wants you to abstain from the love of money, from sexual immorality. This is the will of God. 98% of the will of God is revealed to you; do it. When you do it, God will show you the 2% that are very specific for you. But if you do not obey the things that God has shown us already in

---

43 Acts 9:6.

44 1 Thessalonians 4:3.

the Scriptures, why would we think that He would reveal to us any further information. God will tell you, "Go, and do what you know first, then I will let you know the rest."

4. Seek godly input

Seek godly input. You need to have godly, Christian, spiritually mature mentors, like your spiritual father and Church servant. You need to have mentors in your life to help you, to guide you. Even bishops and clergy have their own mentors, and have their spiritual fathers, to whom they go and ask for guidance and help in making decisions. In the Book of Proverbs, it says, "Where there is no counsel, the people fall; but in the multitude of counselors there is safety."[45] The Church is designed to help us greatly with this. God did not ask us to worship Him as individuals, but He wants us to worship Him in a community, and He called this community "the Church." And He made the Church to be His body—the body of Christ. I encourage you to be in church every single time the doors are open. This will lead you to be more involved with godly people and with the community of the believers, and this will help you more and more to discover and to discern the will of God.

---

45 Proverbs 11:14.

5. Be attentive to the gifts that God gave you

As we have said, God has a plan for each one of us, even before our creation. Therefore, God created you to fulfill a specific role in this world. God did not say, "You know what, today I will create one thousand people, and that is it—haphazardly." No, each one of us is created for a certain purpose, a certain goal, and there is no one else who can completely achieve that for which God has purposely created you to do. St. Peter says, "As each one has received a gift, minister it to one another, as good stewards of the manifold grace of God."[46] God has gifted each one of us to perform a special mission. Therefore, when I know my gift, this will be the will of God for me. Pay attention to how God has gifted you. His plan, and His will for you, is directly related to the gift He has given you. See what your gifts are, and then it will make it very easy to know the will of God for you.

6. Listen to God in prayer

Our prayers are often like a monologue, not rather a dialogue. As we have already said that there are two types of prayer. In the first type, which is wrong, I make the decisions, and I say this is my will in my life and then I am asking God to execute my will for my life. We start our prayer by saying, "God I want this

---

46 1 Peter 4:10.

and that," and then we conclude by saying, "Hear us when we pray thankfully, 'Our Farther who art in heaven,'" and then we leave. It is like you enter into the dean's office and submit a request, and before he answers your request, you leave the office. So, he does not find you to tell you, "Yes" or "No," or what is his plan for you. You go to your professor and tell him "I want to know what you want me to do in this research," and before he answers you, you leave the office. We often do likewise with God: I make decisions and choices about my will, how I want to live my life, and I ask God to execute them for me. But the second type of prayer, which is the right way of prayer, is the prayer of St. Paul. When God appeared to him on the road to Damascus, St. Paul asked the Lord, "Lord, what do You want me to do?"[47] We are created for Him. Therefore, we should ask God every day, "What do You want me to do today? What is Your will for me? What is Your purpose for me?" And St. Paul followed the will of God. You read in the Book of Acts that they went to a certain city, but the Holy Spirit forbade them from preaching in that city. They did not go against the will of God, and they turned and went to another city. People did not antagonize the will of God, but followed it, like St. Mary, St. Paul, and the disciples. They followed the will of God. Pray each day, and each time you pray, ask God, "Lord, what do you want me to do?" I assure you that if

---

47 Acts 9:6.

you pray faithfully and sincerely, God will reveal His will to You.

We need to learn from Samuel when he said, "Speak, for Your servant hears."[48] You need to learn how to silence your mind and your heart, to silence your thought, that God may speak, and you may listen to His word. Maybe after you finish your prayer, then on a piece of paper, you can write the questions that you are waiting for God to answer, whether it is about your career, about your job, about relationship, marriage, monasticism, consecration. It can be one or two questions, or more; write all of them and then sit in silence waiting for God to speak to you. Be assured that when you train yourself, then an idea or a thought will come to your mind, which you have never thought about, and it will give you peace. This is a strong indicator that this is from God. God answers us in different ways. I personally get many of my answers during the Divine Liturgy. For example, I am praying about a subject—I perhaps have an issue in a church, or I am looking for a candidate for the priesthood for this church, and so on—and I am praying for this and leaving it before God; and then during the Divine Liturgy, an idea comes to mind to solve this issue, or a name I had never thought about, who can be a candidate for this church. Very frequently I personally receive the answers during the Divine Liturgy. And I feel very peaceful about it. Therefore,

---

48   1 Samuel 3:10.

try to listen, train yourself to listen to the voice of God. The Lord said in the Gospel, "My sheep hear My voice, and I know them, and they follow Me."[49]

7. Listen to your heart

Listen to your heart. In psalm 37, David the prophet says, "Delight yourself also in the LORD, and He shall give you the desires of your heart. Commit your way to the LORD, trust also in Him, and He shall bring it to pass."[50] "Delight yourself in the Lord" means, "walk with God happily," as the psalmist says, "I was glad when they said to me, 'Let us go into the house of the LORD.'"[51] When you delight yourself in the Lord, God will give you the desire of your heart. When you are close to Him, He will shape your desires, so your desires will be the things which God has already planned for you. Now, your desires will match His will. God will give you the desire of your heart, and also when you trust in Him, He will make this desire to be actualized; nevertheless, the key point is that you delight yourself in the Lord.

8. Examine the circumstances

Take a look at the circumstances. As I have already said, God closes doors and opens other doors. In the

---

49 John 10:27.

50 Psalms 37:4–5.

51 Psalms 122:1.

Book of Acts, we see how God closed some doors to St. Paul and opened others:

> Now when they had gone through Phrygia and the region of Galatia, they were forbidden by the Holy Spirit to preach the word in Asia. After they had come to Mysia, they tried to go into Bithynia, but the Spirit did not permit them. So passing by Mysia, they came down to Troas. And a vision appeared to Paul in the night. A man of Macedonia stood and pleaded with him, saying, "Come over to Macedonia and help us." Now after he had seen the vision, immediately we sought to go to Macedonia, concluding that the Lord had called us to preach the gospel to them.[52]

When they were forbidden by the Holy Spirit, they did not resist. If God did not want them to preach here, then they went to another city. When they tried to go into Bithynia, and the Spirit did not permit them, what did they do? They went to Troas. And after St. Paul saw a vision of a Macedonian man, he concluded that the Lord wanted him to preach in Macedonia.

So, examine the circumstances around you. Perhaps the job for which you have applied several times is not God's plan for you to get. You may need

---

52 Acts 16:6–10.

to apply in another company, for another job. You need to look at the circumstances. Yes, there are some doors which will be closed, but this does not mean that God does not like you, God hates you, God rejects you, God does not love you. It does not mean all of these. It can simply mean that this is not the will of God for you. Look at the open doors. But, also, I want to warn you here that not every open door is necessarily the will of God. That is why you need to follow the mentioned steps not only this one step.

I remember a story about Pope Kyrillos VI. During the early ministry of Pope Kyrillos, some priests were against the Sunday school ministry. They literally closed the doors of their churches to the Sunday school servants, to prevent them from teaching Sunday school. So, a group of Sunday school servants went and complained to Pope Kyrillos. As usual when there is something we do not like, we go and complain. Pope Kyrillos told them, "Yes indeed, the Lord said, 'The harvest is small, and the laborers are plenty.'" Does the verse say so? The verse says the opposite, "The harvest truly is plentiful, but the laborers are few."[53] But Pope Kyrillos reversed the verse. They did not understand what he meant, so they said, "What do you mean by saying that the harvest is small?" He said, "Now I have many laborers in front of me, but they do not have a place to serve." Therefore, they asked him, "Would Your

---

53 Matthew 9:37.

Holiness elaborate?" He told them, "Yes, go to the villages, if the churches in the cities are closed to you, go and serve in the villages." This was the beginning of the Village Ministry in Egypt. No priests used to go to the villages, and the Christians there were Christian by name only. Then Sunday school servants started to go to the villages and do service there. So, in the cities, there were closed doors, but in the villages, there were open doors. Now when you ask about the Village Ministry in the Church, it is a huge ministry. So, God allowed the doors of the churches to be closed, in order for this ministry to start.

9. Use the gift of the mind

God gave us the mind and the intellect, and this is a blessing which we received. In the visible creation, only the human being has this blessing of thinking. If God gave us the mind and the intellect, then we need to use it. Here is a simple way for using it: if you have three or four choices from which you need to choose, then make a table and write all these choices. Then try to fill this table over ten or fifteen days, writing the pros and cons under each choice. As you are praying, as you are asking guidance from spiritual, godly, wise people, as you are asking yourself, 'What would Jesus do?'—then you start filling this table. For example, if I am confused between monasticism and consecration, and I do not know which one I should choose, write the pros and cons of each way—of each choice—and develop it. As we said, do not do it in one session, because thoughts will come to your mind perhaps over ten days or two weeks. And at the end, when you look at this table, it will be clear to you. What will guide you? What is the decision that keeps you closer to God? Because as we agreed in the beginning, "This is the will of God, your sanctification."[54]. So, if you want to be like St. Mary, if you want to be a member in the family of God, His brother, His sister, His mother, do the will of God. After you have gone through the steps we spoke about—do the revealed, common will of God; pray and ask about what He wants you to do; have the mind of Christ; seek spiritual guidance from godly, wise people—then use your mind to compare between all the choices in order to see which choice will keep you sanctified, because this is the will of God: your sanctification.

---

54   1 Thessalonians 4:3.

6

Concluding Remarks

Obedience to the will of God gives true joy

Happiness and joy come only from doing God's will, because you are created for a certain task, and you will never be happy unless you know this purpose and live for that purpose. People who do not discover their purpose, will not live happily in their life. It says in the Book of Proverbs, "He who heeds the word wisely will find good, and whoever trusts in the Lord, happy is he."[55] When you trust in God—in His will for you—you will be happy and blessed. Also, in the gospel of St. John, the Lord said, "If you know these things, blessed are you if you do them."[56] That is to say, "If you know My will, blessed are you if you do it." Therefore,

---

55 Proverbs 16:20.
56 John 13:17.

knowledge is not enough; you will be blessed when you do them. In the Psalms, David the prophet says, "Oh, taste and see that the LORD is good; blessed is the man who trusts in Him!"[57] Following the way of God shows trust, that we trust God; and when we trust Him, we will be blessed; we will be happy.

In psalm 119, which we pray in the first watch in the Midnight Hour of the Agpeya and is the longest psalm in the Scripture, it says, "Blessed are the undefiled in the way, who walk in the law of the LORD! Blessed are those who keep His testimonies, who seek Him with the whole heart!"[58] When we seek God and walk in His way and according to His will, we will be blessed. Another verse in the Psalms says, "Blessed is every one who fears the LORD, who walks in His ways."[59] Walking in the way of God means walking in the will of God. In the Book of Revelation, it says, "Blessed are those who do His commandments, that they may have the right to the tree of life, and may enter through the gates into the city."[60] The commandment of God is His will, because when God commands us to do something, that is His will. Those, who do the will of God will have the right to the tree of life, and may enter the city of Jerusalem. We said that God has a plan for you, and His plan is perfect. As the Lord Jesus

---

57 Psalms 34:8.
58 Psalms 119:1–2.
59 Psalms 128:1.
60 Revelation 22:14.

Christ did the will of the Father, God wants us to do His will; and God will give you the wisdom to know His will and to perform His will. Also true joy and happiness come from the will of God.

Obedience to His will brings blessings

Why we should discover the will of God? Because obedience to the will of God will bring blessings. As we read in the Book of Isaiah:

> Thus says the LORD, your Redeemer, the Holy One of Israel: "I am the LORD your God, who teaches you to profit, who leads you by the way you should go. Oh, that you had heeded My commandments! Then your peace would have been like a river, and your righteousness like the waves of the sea."[61]

Obedience to the will of God will bring me many blessings; my peace will be like a river; my righteousness will be like the waves of the sea.

This book offers some points on why it is important to discover and follow the will of God, and how to do so. For God has a plan; His plan is perfect. The Lord Jesus Christ Himself did the will of the Father. And God will give you wisdom both to discover and to execute His plan, which results in true happiness. Unreserved surrender to

---

61 Isaiah 48:17–18.

His will is needed, and so God will lead us through the Scripture, through opening and closing doors, through the counsel of our spiritual father and through godly people. All the time God is preparing and directing us toward His will, and He will send us certain signs to confirm His will for us. God's peace is a strong indicator, that we are walking in His will. God may lead us one step at a time, but obedience to the will of God will bring us many blessings. Our peace will be like a river, our righteousness will be like the waves of the sea.

Guiding Questions for Reflection

1. Are you truly open to going wherever God leads you? Or are you coming to God to simply obtain approval for your own plans?

2. What do you need to do to fully surrender your desires and be open to God's will?

3. Looking back at your life, have you ever experienced a time when God was guiding you in a specific direction, but you did not realize it until much later?

4. How is God reassuring you as you make choices and take steps of faith right now?

5. What are the decisions and choices you are facing right now in your life?

Write them down and pray about them, and ask faithful friends to pray with you, as you are going through these steps to know the will of God.

Guiding Questions for Reflection

Every time we pray the Lord's prayer "Thy will be done," let us say to Him genuinely and sincerely, "We are asking for Your will to be done in our life."

Questions and Answers

Q1. If people left all in God's hand, then they will stop trying for a specific goal, saying, "Oh, it is not working; I will not try any more. It must not be the will of God." How do we know whether this specific goal just needs more work, or it is not God's will?

A1. As I said, if you follow all the steps I mentioned, you will be able to know God's will. For example, St. Paul knew that it is God's will to preach in Macedonia, so do you think his preaching in Macedonia was very easy? No, in Philippi he was thrown in prison; he was stoned. But knowing this was the will of God in his life to preach there, he endured all of this. He did not simply say, "It is not the will of God," and then abandoning it. For example, if somebody is called to the priesthood or monasticism, first you pray and follow certain steps to make sure that this is the will of God. Once you know that it is the will of God, and you become a monk, a nun, or a priest, then, yes, you will face many difficulties and challenges. You are not going to say, "It is not the will of God; I will go back." No. I will know for sure that it is the will of God through the steps that I mentioned. Once I know the will of God and I have peace in my heart about it, then I will pursue it regardless of what challenges I face.

Q2. How can I be faithful in doing God's will, for His will is not the easy way, nor is it the simplest? The struggle is in not knowing why God wants us to do what He calls us for.

A2. Perhaps we do not know why God wants me to do this, but what we know for certain is that if we do it, we will be blessed, happy, joyful, and at peace. That is what we know for sure. At the end, it is your choice. If you choose not to be faithful in doing God's will, then you will lose this happiness and joy and peace. Does it need a struggle? Yes, definitely it needs a struggle, but God will not leave you in your struggle. He will be with you, supporting you, giving you the wisdom that you need, entering with you into all your pains and struggles and difficulties. He will never forsake you nor leave you. With this trust, it will be easy for you to be faithful, to do God's will.

Q3. How do you know when a door is closed by God?

A3. As I told you, you will not have peace about this way. When you ask many people, they will not be comfortable about this way. As I told you, God is not the author of confusion. God will send you certain signs or verses or messages, assuring you that this is not the way. When you try to knock on this door or to pursue it, you will find may challenges. So, when you put all these things together, then you will know that this door is not for you. It is closed.

Q4. How does one know what is the gift that God has given them? Is there something that is supposed to be revealed at a certain time? Is there anything one can do to speed up the process of finding our gift?

A4. Yes, you can pray about it and God will help you, to reveal your gift to you. Also, you can listen to the feedback other people give you. For example, people will say to you, "You have leadership qualities"; "You know, when I talk to you, I feel comfortable," so perhaps your gift is counseling, or you may be good at administration. So listen to the feedback from other people. I remember one time I was giving a workshop about the gift of the Holy Spirit. There was a group of twelve people, so I asked everyone to write down what they believe that their own gift is. We read about gifts in the Scriptures. There are four references to the gifts: Romans 12, 1 Corinthians 12, 1 Peter 4, and Ephesians 4. We wrote a list of all the gifts mentioned in the Scriptures. I said to them, "I want everyone to write the gift that they believe they have." Then I asked everyone to write the gift they believe that the rest of the members of the group have. I believe this person has this gift, that person has that gift, and so on. So each one received feedback from the eleven persons who were in the room, beside what they believed their own gift was. So listen to the feedback, pray about it, and see what God made you good at. This will be your gift.

Q5. Does the will of God include punishment?

A5. Punishment is a consequence of our sins. God said to Adam, "If you eat from this tree, then you shall surely die." So, it is not the will of God that we perish or be punished, but if you choose not to follow His will, then there will be consequences for not following His will.

Q6. If God's will is sovereign, and we ourselves cannot change anything of God's will, then do we have free will?

A6. When we speak about the will of God, there is the sovereign will of God and the prescriptive will of God. You did not focus on the prescriptive will of God. I gave you example on the sovereign will of God, like the crucifixion, to die for the salvation of the world. This is the will of God, which will be done no matter what. But when we speak about the prescriptive will of God, we said that God gave you a commandment as He gave to Adam and Eve, but by their free will they chose not to follow the will of God and ate of the forbidden tree. So, we need to think about both sovereign and prescriptive wills of God.

Q7. If we go off God's way and return to Him, will He show His will? And how can we see it during hardship?

A7. Yes, God always desires to let us know His will. If we return back to Him, He will certainly reveal His will to us, and He will make us to see it even during hardship. St. Paul was going against the will of God, but when he returned to God, he knew the will of God in his mind.

Q8. How do we differentiate God's sovereign will and God taking away free will?

A8. God will never take away free will from us. In anything pertaining to you, it is your free will. Even salvation, it is your free will to accept the salvation of the Lord or to reject it. But His sovereign will is to save the whole world. So, what I am trying to say: anything pertaining to you, it is your choice; it is your free will. Anything pertaining to the whole world together, it is pertaining to God's will.

Q9. How do I accept God's will for me gracefully and happily if it is against my will?

A9. If you trust Him and you know that His will is better than your will, whatever He chooses for you on the long run is better than what you choose for yourself. Church history and the Bible inform us that what we choose for ourselves is worse than what God chooses for us. Have confidence in the love of God for you.

Q10. If someone constantly refuses to follow the will of God, how can we help them see the ways of God and bring them back?

A10. God made a rule in Galatians, "Whatever a man sows, that he will also reap."[62] Sometimes we intervene to stop this Divine will. Therefore, when they do something wrong, and you try to spare them the consequences of their wrong decision, then they continue to do what is wrong. In the Parable of the Prodigal Son, the father did not send him money nor food. If the father had sent him money and food, he would never have returned. He suffered the consequences, and this suffering made him return back to his father on his own. This is why we say, "Do not enable

---

62 Galatians 6:7.

them." If somebody refuses to do the will of God, let them suffer the consequences of their wrong choice. Let them suffer, but pray for them, and they will return back.

www.ingramcontent.com/pod-product-compliance
Lightning Source LLC
Chambersburg PA
CBHW031433040426
42444CB00006B/781